Tallinn Travel Guide

Sightseeing, Hotel, Restaurant & Shopping Highlights

Thomas Austin

Copyright © 2014, Astute Press
All Rights Reserved.

No part of this publication may be reproduced, stored in a retrieval system, or transmitted, in any form or by any means without the prior written permission of the publisher, nor be otherwise circulated in any form of binding or cover other than that in which it is published and without similar condition being imposed on the subsequent purchaser.

If there are any errors or omissions in copyright acknowledgements the publisher will be pleased to insert the appropriate acknowledgement in any subsequent printing of this publication.

Although we have taken all reasonable care in researching this book we make no warranty about the accuracy or completeness of its content and disclaim all liability arising from its use

Table of Contents

Tallinn 5
   Culture 6
   Location & Orientation 8
   Climate & When to Visit 10

Sightseeing Highlights 12
   Seaplane Harbour & Estonian Maritime Museum 13
   Tallinn Botanical Garden 14
   Tallinn TV Tower 16
   Estonian Open Air Museum 17
   Alexander Nevsky Cathedral 18
   KGB Museum 19
   Museum of Occupations 20
   City Museum 21
   Kadriog Palace & Art Museum 22
   Kiek in de Kok & Bastion Passages Museum 23
   Old Town 25

Recommendations for the Budget Traveller 27
   Places to Stay 27
      St. Barbara Hotel 27
      L'Ermitage 28
      Hotel Oru 29
      Kalev Spa Hotel 29
      Hotel Euroopa 30
   Places to Eat 31
      Baieri Kelder 31
      Alter Ego 31
      Dominic 32
      Grillhaus Daube 32
      Bistroo Mary 33
   Places to Shop 34
      Kaubamaja 34
      Estonia Handicraft House 34
      Kalev Chocolate Shop 35
      Viru Centre 35
      Town Hall Square 36

Tallinn

Tallinn is the capital of Estonia and is the oldest capital city in northern Europe. The city is the financial, business and technology hub of the Baltic region and The New York Times has called the city the "Silicon Valley on the Baltic Sea." Estonia is one of the smallest countries in Europe and Tallinn's well-preserved buildings and Old World vibe delight its visitors.

Tallinn has become a busy cruise ship port and travel destination because of its mixture of new infrastructure together with its historic old town. Many parts of the city date back to medieval times. Some of the buildings and surrounding areas resemble film sets, with cobblestone streets, churches with domes and spires, architecture from the Middle Ages, and stone city walls.

There are four areas of Tallinn – Toompea, or the Upper Town, with its embassies, government-related structures and residences, All-linn or Lower Town, which includes the Old Town, Kadriorg, the coastal district which includes the Kadriorg Palace, and Pirita, just beyond Kadriorg, where the Olympic marina and the cruise ship port are located.

It's easy to see why nearly two million tourists visit the city yearly and why the Old Town has been placed on the UNESCO list of World Heritage Sites.

Culture

Tallinn was nominated as the 2011 European Capital of Culture and the city has great reverence for art, music and history. Many of the buildings that house museums are themselves of great interest, since they date back to medieval times.

Many people became aware of Tallinn (population 430,000) during the 1980 Summer Olympics. Though the host city for the games was Moscow, Russia, the sailing events took place in Tallinn. The city built a marina especially for the events, and a television tower (Tallinn TV Tower) was erected to enhance telecommunications signals during the Olympic broadcasts. Both of these venues exist today and the TV Tower in particular is now a popular destination for tourists.

Except for sailing-related events Tallinn is not particularly known for its involvement in sports. But they do have a horse show, sometimes twice a year, in the spring and autumn, and it attracts a great number of people. The city is much more interested in music, hosting several events and festivals throughout the year

Estonians feel close ties to Northern European and Scandinavian countries and they have a special bond to the people and culture of Finland, a close neighbor. The fact that the city of Tallinn has elevated its tourist and cultural status is commendable, considering its many military outbreaks and the three major foreign occupations of the city. Some of Tallinn's fortresses date back to the year 1050 when even then the townspeople sought to strike a note of freedom.

From 1918 to 1920, the Soviets occupied the city and dominated the lives of Estonian people. Just as that period ended, the Germans arrived with Nazi's occupying the city during the Holocaust, from 1941-44. Another Soviet takeover occurred just after the Holocaust and lasted more than four decades, until 1991, when the Estonians finally fought for and gained their independence.

During this time, the KGB controlled much of the information being distributed within the city and they had a headquarters in Tallinn, which can be visited today. In 1990, the Soviets attempted to overtake the Tallinn TV Tower that had been built with pride for the Olympics, but the citizens fought back and this was a pivotal moment in turning the tide toward freedom and independence.

Today the city is clean and safe, though as in many tourist cities, visitors are cautioned to beware of pickpockets, especially in the Old Town area. Visitors should check with their own country's government policies for information on the need for a visa to visit Tallinn, but a valid passport is enough documentation to enter Tallinn for people from many countries, including the United States.

The official language is Estonian, with Russian running a close second. Other languages that might be heard are Ukranian, Belarusian and Finnish, although English is spoken to some degree in many shops and restaurants and at most hotels. English is offered as a language choice on guided tours. And at web sites for various attractions, English can be chosen as the language to read the information in, since the web site may have as its original language Estonian. Simply click on the British flag (representing English) or on English, usually in the upper right corner of the web site.

Souvenir seekers should look for hand-crafted items made by Estonians, such as knitted wool sweaters (with folk scenes or characters on them), hats, carved wood items (including beer mugs), hats, candle holders made from local limestone, art, and glassware. Most major credit cards are accepted in shops, restaurants and hotels and for currency, Estonia has adopted the Euro.

Location & Orientation

Tallinn is located on the northern coast of Estonia, near the Gulf of Finland. It is located to the south of Helsinki, Finland, to the east of Stockholm, Sweden, and to the west of St. Petersburg, Russia.

Visitors arriving in the city often come by cruise ship, though a flight into the city is the most popular mode of transportation. Many major airlines fly into the Lemart Meri Tallinn Airport, with SAS and Finnair being the most popular choices. Unlike many other major cities, the airport serving Tallinn is conveniently located only two miles from the heart of the city (Old Town) so this makes for an easy and economical journey to one's hotel.

The #90K bus runs from the airport to the city center every thirty minutes from 8 a.m. to 6 p.m. and is an excellent way to make the transfer. The cost is 2€ ($3) per person. Taxis are also available for the transfer and the fare should run about 7-10€ ($9-13) for the trip. Some reputable taxi companies are Tallink, Tulika, Tallinna and Sobra.

Once in the city, buses travel frequently from one location to the next so seeing the sights is relatively easy. There are also hop-on, hop-off bus tours that take visitors on a brief sightseeing tour of the city and for many people this is a good method for becoming orientated to the surroundings. It is easy to get off the bus and then rejoin it at any of the 18 stops around the city. The primary company providing this service is City Sightseeing, whose web site is www.citysightseeing.ee and whose phone number is 372-655-8328. In and around the Old Town area, visitors can very comfortably travel on foot from one destination to the next.

A wise investment for many people is the Tallinn Card, which should be purchased in advance. Information about the card can be found at www.tourism.tallinn.ee/en or by telephoning the Old Town Information Center at 372-645-7777. The card is popular because it can be used for transportation purposes as well as to gain free admission to more than 40 attractions around town. Purchase of the card also entitles the visitor to a one-hour sightseeing tour and they can choose from three different tours. Discounts are also given to cardholders at various shops in Tallinn.

A 24-hour card costs 24€ ($32) for adults and 12€ ($16) for children. A two-day card is 32€ ($43) for adults and 16€ ($22) for children. The most frequently purchased card is the three-day card, for 40€ ($54) for adults and 20€ ($27) for children. When used wisely and time to coincide with visits to museums or other tourist spots, the savings can be great. The tourism department claims that there are 100 ways to save in Tallinn by using the card.

Climate & When to Visit

Temperatures vary quite a bit in Tallinn, ranging from cold and snowy winters to warm and mild summers. Snow can be expected from December until at least the end of March, with February usually being the coldest month of the year (temperatures about -4°C or 24°F on average). Spring – March through May - is fairly pleasant with temperatures averaging 15°C or 59°F.

The summer months of June through August are the warmest but also the wettest months and rain can be expected at any time during those months. Temperatures average 19-21°C (66-70°F) and July is the warmest of those months overall, with averages of 17°C (63°F) but many times much warmer, meaning into the high 70s or low 80s, Fahrenheit. Humidity is an issue in Tallinn year-round but particularly in the summer months when it might reach 81%. The autumn is very pleasant, with temperatures between 11°C (52°F) to 15°C (59°F).

Most attractions are open year-round but they are also closed, regardless of the time of year, on Mondays for the most part. There is a film festival held in Tallinn each year, attracting entries from around the world. It is held in November or December with a date to be determined yearly. There are many music festivals in the city, in winter and spring. And every five years, the Estonian Song Celebration is held, attracting an average of 90,000 spectators. About 35,000 singers participate. It is best to consult a tourism web site for update festival information (such as www.visitestonia.com).

Though the winter is a fairly cold time to visit, it offers enchanting activities such a jazz festival, an outdoor ice skating rink, and a large Christmas market in Old Town.

Here is a link to information about the current weather in Tallinn: http://www.wunderground.com/weather-forecast/EE/Tallinn.html

Sightseeing Highlights

Most of the city's attractions have individual admission tickets but also offer what they call a "family ticket", which will admit two adults and two children for one admission price. This can be an economical way to visit an attraction. Also visitors who purchased the Tallinn Card will receive free admission to many of the attractions. Check with an attraction's ticketing office prior to buying tickets to make sure that your Tallinn Card's admission is in effect at that location.

Seaplane Harbour & Estonian Maritime Museum

17 Kuti Street/6 Vesilennuki Street
Tallinn 10415, Estonia
372-620-0550
www.seaplaneharbour.com

Estonia's extensive history of sea-related activity is represented well in this museum. The location has been voted the most-visited museum in Estonia. There are historical seaplane hangars which contain the exhibits and memorabilia. This is quite an interactive attraction. Visitors can climb into a submarine from 1930 to get a feeling for what it was like for sailors to live in these vessels while fighting underwater.

As the museum's name would imply, seaplanes are also on display, including a replica of a British seaplane named the Short 184, which was the first to undertake a torpedo attack by air. There is a simulator so that visitors can again get a sense of actually being in a plane that hovers on the water. A steam ship is on display that is the largest in the world and was used in two World Wars. An intriguing display is the wreck of the Maasilinn, a ship found in the waters of Estonia in 1980. The ship dates back to the Middle Ages, sometime after 1550.

Think about visiting Fat Margaret, too. This isn't a socially improper thing to say – Fat Margaret is an artillery tower from medieval days, and its name apparently came from a nickname soldiers gave to one of the larger cannons they used.

At various times Fat Margaret was used to store gun powder and supplies. It was also used as a prison at one point. There are also special exhibits at the museum from time to time. A recent exhibit included a display of items and photos from the Titanic.

There is a café (Café Maru) on the premises that many visitors take advantage of for Nordic or Estonian foods and the fact that they can dine while being right in the middle of the museum. Items include various salads, a fish platter, or a fairly common choice in Estonia – pig's ears! Prices for most items are between 6€ ($8) and 8€ ($11).

The museum is open Tuesday through Sunday from 10 a.m. to 7 p.m. Tickets are 10€ ($13) for Adults, 5€ ($7) for children and students. Family tickets are 20€ ($27). Fat Margaret requires a separate admission which is 5€ ($7) for adults, 3€ ($4) for children and 10€ ($13) for a family ticket.

Tallinn Botanical Garden

Kloostrimesta tee 52
Tallinn 11913, Estonia
372-606-2679
www.tallinnbotanicgarden.org

Records indicate that the idea for a botanical garden in Tallinn first began during the 1860s. It "only" took 100 years for the idea to come to fruition, since this location was originally opened in 1961 as a project of Estonia's Academy of Sciences, to study and preserve natural plants of the area.
But the 300-acre property close to the city center was eventually open to the public and presents a dazzling array of local and foreign plants and other greenery.

Depending on the season, visitors can expect to see lilies, lilacs, a rose garden, an arboretum, a rock garden, a pine forest, many variations of cacti, an iron ore site, a grassland area, an oak forest, ferns, birch and alder trees and a swamp area. Fifteen distinct settings of landscapes are included, with thousands of plants. There are two nature trails that provide an easy walk while enjoying many of the greenery displays.

This site is a short distance and an easy walk from the Tallinn TV Tower and visitors may want to combine a visit here with a visit to the tower. Combination tickets may be purchased for both venues for 9€ ($12) for adults, 7€ ($9) for children and students, or 18€ ($24) for families.

For single tickets just to the botanical garden, tickets cost 3.5€ ($5) adults, 2.5€ ($3) students and seniors, or 6€ ($8) for a family ticket. Visitors may also purchase a guided tour if desired, for a fee of 45€ ($61) for a party of up to 10 people. The grounds are open from 9 a.m. to 5 pm. daily.

Tallinn TV Tower

Kloostrimesta tee 58A
Tallinn 11913, Estonia
372-686-3005
www.teletorn.ee/en

It won't be difficult for visitors to find the TV Tower, since it's the tallest building not only in Tallinn but in all of Estonia. The tower was built to provide better transmission during the 1980 Olympics, which were held for the most part in Moscow, but Tallinn was host city for the sailing events.

There is a darker history to the tower, however. In 1991, Soviet troops attempted to take over control of Tallinn, including the control tower and therefore, they would control telecommunications in the city. But the Estonian people defended the tower, the city and the country and Estonia won its freedom.

There are several technological exhibits here and many are interactive. There is a mini TV studio and a part of the tower has a glass floor, where visitors can actually look down at the city below. A gift shop offers souvenirs and children will be entertained by a frequent story time event (check the web site for updated information). The mascot, named Eti, who resembles a space alien, will greet children and adults alike when they arrive.

For the more daring visitors a special feature exists that is called Edgewalk. Imagine walking and perching on the ledge of the 22nd floor of the tower! Four people at a time are able to be guided through this adventure, and while they are attached with a safety harness, it is still not for the fearful. Height, age and health restrictions are posted at the web site.

In spite of the risk, thrill seekers have been lining up to do this and to have their photo taken in the process of standing or walking on the edge. A separate ticket for this adventure costs 20€ ($27). Admission to the tower is 7€ ($9) for adults and 4€ ($5) for children or seniors. A family ticket is 15€ ($20).

There is a combination ticket available to visit the nearby Botanical Garden as well as the TV Tower – those tickets are 9€ ($12) for adults and children. The tower is open October through April from 11 a.m. to 6 p.m. on Wednesday through Monday.

Estonian Open Air Museum

Vabashumuuseumi tee 12
Tallinn 13521, Estonia
372-654-9100
www.evm.ee/keel/en

This location is quite unique. Instead of bringing artifacts indoors, the actual grounds themselves are the museum. The location has preserved country village life by maintaining, among other highlights, 12 farms, a church, a tavern, a schoolhouse, a mill, a firehouse, and a handicraft shop – all in their natural form.

They exist just 15 minutes from the center of town but are years apart from modern society in terms of appearance. It is a way for tourists to walk around the countryside as it once was. Seventy-two village buildings from old Tallinn were actually moved from their earlier spots, delivered to this site and re-built to form one village within easy walking distance from one building to another.

The site is open from September 29 to April 22 from 10 a.m. to 5 p.m. and from April 23 to September 28 from 10 a.m. to anywhere from 6 to 8 p.m. depending on visitor traffic. Admission varies depending on the season. From September 29 to April 22 admission is 4€ adults ($5), 2€ ($3) for students, children and seniors, a family ticket is 8€ ($11) and children under 7 are admitted free. From April 23 to September 28 admission is 6€ ($8) adults, 3€ ($4) for seniors, students and children, and the family ticket is 12€ ($16).

Alexander Nevsky Cathedral

Lossiplats 10
Tallinn 10130, Estonia
372-644-3484
www.teelistekirikud.ekn.ee/2012/en_kirik

Regardless of one's religion, a visit to this cathedral is worth a visit for the beauty of the building, inside and out. This is an orthodox cathedral, located on the hill of Toompea, in the Old Town section of Tallinn and it is the largest cathedral with cupolas in Tallinn. Construction on it was completed in 1900 and it was built in traditional Russian style with onion domes, making it have a striking appearance.

The cathedral was named in honor of St. Alexander Nevsky, who in 1242 defeated the Teutonic Knights during what was known as the Battle of the Ice on nearby Lake Peipus. The cathedral is not without controversy.

Estonians were so bitter about Russian domination and oppression in their country that in 1924 there was a movement to have the cathedral demolished. Ironically, the movement could not raise enough funds for the demolition so the project never happened.

Today, now that Estonia is a free country, the citizens of Tallinn appreciate the cathedral. Its bell tower features 11 bells of all sizes and the interior has many elaborate mosaics and statues of saints. The cathedral is open Monday through Friday and on Sunday from 8 a.m. to 7 p.m. and on Saturday from 8 a.m. – 8 p.m. Admission is free and visitors are asked to be respectful and not disturb any services that may be in progress during a visit.

KGB Museum

Sokos Hotel Viru – Viru Valjak 4
Tallinn 10111, Estonia
372-680-9300
www.sokoshotels.ee

For most people, the KGB is something they've only read about in history books or seen portrayed in spy movies. But it was a very real force and played a role in the history of Tallinn during the Soviet occupation. The hotel itself was built in 1972 and the top floor was used as a listening post for the KGB, for "national security" reasons.

Once the Soviets were defeated and departed in 1991, the items left behind were preserved as a way to remind Estonians and those around the world of what was once part of Estonian life.

Listening equipment remains, the radio room is intact, a complaint book was left behind, where names and addresses of supposedly suspicious (anti-Soviet) residents were recorded, and there are photos of the time period as well as other artifacts, such as papers bearing the common Soviet/KGB phrase "There is nothing here". Visit the bar in the hotel to see the postcard set on display (and for sale) bearing this term.

The museum is open on Tuesday through Sunday from 10 a.m. to 5:30 p.m. and admission is 8€ ($11) flat rate for a guided tour (required). Call in advance to book the tour. The admission includes free entry to the night club Café Amigo on the same day as your tour of the museum. Tour times vary depending on the language spoken.

Museum of Occupations

Toompea Street 8, corner Toompea and Kaarli Boulevard
Tallinn 10142, Estonia
372-668-0250
www.okupatsioon.ee/en

Another museum worthy of a visit and pertaining to military occupations is the Museum of Occupations. It may not be the most cheerful of sites and the overall feeling is a bit oppressive, but that is more or less the intention since it provides information about the three times that Tallinn was occupied by outside forces.

The museum has a good selection of photos, videos and artifacts including clothing, prison doors, documents, and letters, as well as several statues of famous Russians and dictators.

The museum is an eerie reminder of how a city can change when foreigners invade and take it over. It is also, though, a testimony to the strength of Estonia to survive and restore itself to independent statehood. Both Soviet occupations are represented as well as the German invasion during the Holocaust.

Allow enough time to experience the museum. It may be relatively small, but the videos will take time and are well worth the effort. The museum is open Tuesday through Sunday from 11 a.m. to 6 p.m. Admission is 4€ ($5) for adults, 2€ ($3) for students and seniors. An audio guide is available in several languages.

City Museum

Vene Street 17
Tallinn 10123, Estonia
372-615-5183
www.linnamuuseum.ee/linnamuseum/en

The historical experience begins even from the outside of the museum, since the building it is housed in dates back to medieval times, somewhere in the 14th century. For many centuries it was owned by prominent citizens such as merchants and town officials. It was refurbished in 1965 and became a museum. Many centuries of Tallinn's history is revealed here, from its very earliest days until after the freedom of the city following Soviet occupation in 1991.

Among the 154,000 items on display are ancient spears and other weapons, books, manuscripts, crafts, coats of arms, costumes, jewelry, treasure chests, ceramics, tiles, leather, glass, pewter, toys, art and photos. Some of the items, especially those from the 4th through the 13th century, were discovered during archaeology digs.

It is open from March through October on Wednesdays to Mondays, 10 a.m. to 6 p.m. and in November through February on Wednesday through Monday from 10 a.m. to 5 p.m. Admission is 3.20€ ($4) for adults, 2€ ($3) for seniors and family tickets are 6.40€ ($7). Guided tours are offered for 32€ ($43). You need to obtain a permit in advance to take photos here, and no flash can be used.

Kadriog Palace & Art Museum

A. Weizenbergi 37
Tallinn 10127, Estonia
372-606-6400
www.kadriorumuseum.ee/en

 The term "kadriorg" means, roughly translated, "Catherine's Valley", which refers to the view and area upon which this palace is located. The "Catherine" in question is the wife of Tsar Peter the Great, who had this Baroque-style home built as a gift to her, to serve as their summer residence in 1725. The effect is somewhat like the palace of Versailles in Paris. There is much gilded beauty here and the grounds, called Kadriog Park, are beautifully maintained and lavish.

There is a swan pond, a gazebo, a fountain and a Japanese garden, as well, and it is a relaxing spot to spend quiet time. Back inside, the art museum in housed within the palace walls. Early foreign art (Russian, European, Dutch, German and Italian) is displayed – a total of 9000 pieces of art in all, from the 16th through the 20th century.

Before opening as a museum, the palace was used as an office for the heads of state. Later, a presidential palace was built to serve that purpose. Visits may take place from Thursday to Sunday from 10 a.m. to 5 p.m. and it is open on Wednesday from 10 a.m. to 8 p.m. Tickets are 4.80€ ($6) for adults, 2.80€ ($4) for seniors and students. Family tickets are 9.30€ ($13).

Kiek in de Kok & Bastion Passages Museum

Komandandi 2
Tallinn 10130, Estonia
372-644-6686
www.linnamuuseum.ee/kiek/en

The name of this 5-story location comes from the expression "peep into the kitchen", which is what soldiers in this artillery tower could do with homes nearby. It actually gives a great view of much of the city. The watchtower still has cannonballs from 1577 embedded into its outer surface. It helped protect Tallinn for centuries, dating back as far as 1219.

A video and sound effects are just two ways visitors are able to immerse themselves in the history of major military times for Estonia.

There are two separate admissions for the attractions here. The Kiek in de Kok ticket is 4.08€ ($6) for adults, 2.60€ ($4) for seniors and students, and family tickets are 9€ ($12).

Guided tours are offered in English for 32€ ($43). But the area can easily be explored independently. The next attraction, the Bastion Passages Museum (and Tunnels) allows visitors rare access to the tunnels that were built under the old city. It tells how and why they were built and when citizens hid in the tunnels.

The tunnels were primarily used from 1630 to the 1700s and were also used as a means for soldiers and supplies to move about underground. The tunnels were used in the 1930s as an air raid shelter during the first Soviet invasion. They were fairly elaborately furnished with bedrooms, toilets, electricity and running water. A note about visiting the tunnels: they are not recommended for children under 7.

Also, visitors should be aware that some of the steps are steep and good walking shoes with non-slip soles are necessary. The temperature in the tunnels is cold, like a cave – dress warmly and blankets will be handed out as well.

Tours of the tunnels are booked for groups only so call ahead to be included. For the tunnel tour call 372-644-6686. The tunnel ticket is 5.80€ ($8) for adults, 3.20€ ($4) for seniors and students and a family ticket is 11.5€ ($16). A joint ticket to each attraction is also available – consult the web site for updated information as this fluctuates. The location is open from March to October on Tuesday to Sunday, 10:30 a.m. to 6 p.m. and from November to February on Tuesday to Sunday from 10 a.m. to 5:30 p.m.

Old Town

City Centre, Tallinn 10111, Estonia
www.visitestonia.com

Visitors may feel they are stepping onto a movie set when visiting what is no doubt the most popular tourist site in Tallinn – the area known as Old Town. This is the heart of the city and has retained its medieval look from its early days, which means the buildings are indeed old, dating back from the 13th to 16th century.

The cobblestone streets wind past restaurants, shops and open-air markets. Street lamps light the way as it gets dark outside. The Tallinn Town Hall is in this area as are several galleries and cathedrals, including the Alexander Nevsky Cathedral. The neighborhood is enclosed by the city wall and features colorful homes with courtyards, and houses with gables.

Many points of interest and tourist attractions are located right near Old Town, but enough time should be allowed just roaming the picture-perfect streets.

Recommendations for the Budget Traveller

Places to Stay

St. Barbara Hotel

Roosikrantsi Hotell Ov, Roosikrantski 2a
Tallinn 10119, Estonia
372-640-0040
www.stbarbara.ee/en

This hotel is centrally located in the Old Town section of Tallinn and is therefore near many attractions and several are within walking distance, saving on taxi fare or bus fare. It is a small hotel (53 rooms) and the rooms are quite spacious by European standards. There is a buffet breakfast included in the room rate and the rooms have hair dryers, free Internet service and TVs. There is a popular German-themed restaurant named Baieri Kelder located on the premises (in the cellar) as well as a bar and lounge. Double rooms (two beds) are priced from 100€ ($135), triple rooms or family suites (a queen bed and a twin) begin at 130€ ($175) and a junior suite begins at 150€ ($202).

L'Ermitage

Toompuies tee 19
Tallinn 10137, Estonia
372-699-6400
www.lermitagehotel.ee

This 91-room hotel is in the center of town, a five-minute walk from Old Town. It offers modern rooms, a sauna, a jacuzzi, free WiFi, iron and ironing board upon request, air conditioning, TV, hair dryers, room service, a bar and lounge, mini safes and in some rooms, coffee/tea makers. The hotel has just undergone a renovation and has added quite a few new rooms so visitors might inquire about one of those rooms when booking.

The new rooms offer bathrobes, slippers, air conditioning with hand controls, and coffee and tea makers in every room. They often run specials so it is advised that visitors check out the web site before making reservations. They also have packages available, particularly the romance package which includes wine, a fruit platter, breakfast and dinner at the hotel restaurant, and late check-out. Standard or business-class rooms begin at 54€ ($73). A superior room with breakfast is available from 70€ ($94).

Hotel Oru

Narva Maantee 120B
Tallinn 10127, Estonia
372-603-3300
www.oruhotel.ee

This small hotel has an intimate feel to it with only 50 rooms. It is located in the beautiful Park Kadriorg (Kadriorg Palace) area, near the city's waterfront and about 10 minutes from Old Town.

If a visit is planned during one of the years that the Song Festival is occurring (once every 5 years), this is a location to keep in mind since it is very near the festival's location. Rooms feature TV, WiFi, and a free buffet breakfast, and begin at 99€ ($133) for two beds.

Kalev Spa Hotel

QU Kalevi, Veekaskus Aia 18
Tallinn 10111, Estonia
372-649-3300
www.kalevspa.ee

This hotel is not only close to many attractions but also very close to the airport, for convenience. The rooms include a mini bar, room service availability, a hair dryer, iron and ironing board in many rooms, WiFi, and there is a safe deposit box, pool, restaurant, gym and sauna on the property. Massages can also be booked through the hotel desk and are reasonably priced.

There is a small water park at the hotel and visitors have complimentary use of it during their stay. The water park includes water slides, tube slides, and children's pools. Rooms begin at 76€ ($102) for two beds.

Hotel Euroopa

Paadi 5
Tallinn 10115, Estonia
372-669-9777
www.euroopa.ee

This hotel prides itself on its many amenities, including a relaxing waterfall in the lobby, the availability of a safe deposit box, a sauna and a gym, a bar and lounge, room service, a beauty salon, and in the rooms, TVs, blackout curtains, air conditioning, an ironing board and iron and a hair dryer. They also have a mini shuttle bus available that visitors may book to take them to various sites, rather than taking a city bus or taxi. Rooms start at 75€ ($101) and include breakfast.

A cute touch here is that their "mascot" at the hotel is a lamb. Visitors will find a small stuffed lamb perched on their bed upon arrival, welcoming them to the hotel. For a small fee it can be taken home as a souvenir.

Places to Eat

Baieri Kelder

Roosikrantsi 2A
Tallinn 10119, Estonia
372-640-0045
www.stbarbara.ee/en/baieri-kelder

This German restaurant is located in the cellar of the St. Barbara hotel and is popular with locals and tourists. Favorites include snacks (such as bread, pretzels, a cheese plate or a sausage plate) with beer for 1.90€ ($3) to 9.50€ ($13), soups for 5-7€ ($7-9), and entire meals of fish, beef or pork are served, from 9.50€ to 12.50€ ($13-17). A real crowd pleaser is the typically German sausage and sauerkraut plate for 9.50€ ($13). Pies are baked on the premises and run from 4-5€ ($6-7). The restaurant is open Monday through Saturday from noon till 11 p.m. and Sunday from 2 p.m. till 11 p.m.

Alter Ego

Rosseni 8
Tallinn 10111, Estonia
372-456-0339
www.altergo.ee

This restaurant was voted one of the 15 best restaurants in the Baltic or Russia for 2012 and one of the top 5 restaurants in Estonia.

Their soup and salad choices are extensive and average 6-12€ ($8-16). Main courses are plentiful and are in the 11-20€ range ($15-27). The restaurant is open Sunday through Thursday from noon to 10:30 p.m. and on Friday and Saturday from noon till 11 p.m.

Dominic

Vene 10
Tallinn 10123, Estonia
372-641-0400
www.restoran.ee

The building that houses this restaurant is in the heart of Old Town and dates back to 1374. The restaurant features main dishes of fish, chicken, duck or beef in the 15€ ($20) price range. Salads usually cost 7-10€ ($9-13) and desserts are 4€ ($5) on average. The restaurant is open Monday through Saturday from noon till midnight and on Sunday from noon till 9 p.m.

Grillhaus Daube

Ruutli 11
Tallinn 10130, Estonia
372-645-5531
www.daube.ee

This restaurant has a great selection of grilled foods. Appetizers include salads with chicken, soups, tiger shrimp and smoked trout in the 4-6€ ($5-8) price range.

Main dishes include vegetables grilled in a wok, pasta with salmon, salmon with rice, ribs, or steak and run from 7-18€ ($9-24). The restaurant is open daily from noon to 11 p.m.

Bistroo Mary

Paldioki mnt 4
Tallinn 10111, Estonia
372-628-8150
www.meritonhotels.com/bistroo_mary

This restaurant is located inside the Meriton Hotel in the city center. They only serve lunch (12-3 p.m. daily) and are very popular. They boast of offering the "largest schnitzels in Estonia." (Schnitzels are made with tenderized meat, coated in eggs, flour and bread crumbs and then fried). They also serve sandwiches, pastries, fish and ships and salads – all part of a lunch buffet that costs 20€ ($27) but can contain as many items as you wish.

Places to Shop

Kaubamaja

Gonsiori 2
Tallinn 10143, Estonia
372-667-3100
www.kaujbamaja.ee.en

This shopping center features fashion for men, women and children, home decorations, beauty items and toys, among many other items. It is a popular shopping location with locals so not every item is "touristy", and the center is open daily from 9 a.m. to 7 p.m.

Estonia Handicraft House

Pikk 22
Tallinn 10013, Estonia
372-631-4076
www.crafts.ee

Locally-crafted items are the key to this location's appeal. Whether it's home decorations, fabrics, clothing or other small items, this is a good place to pick up an item that will be a reminder of the people of Estonia who created it. They are open Monday through Saturday from 10 a.m. to 6 p.m. and on Sunday from 10 a.m. to 5 p.m.

Kalev Chocolate Shop

Roseni 7 – Rotermann Qtr
Tallinn 10111, Estonia
372-54 52 58 29
www.kalev.eu.en

Visitors with a sweet tooth might want to spend some time at this store that is the biggest and oldest confectionery business in Estonia. They have been in operation since 1806 and produce sweet biscuits in addition to the candies.

Some of the candy is not chocolate – they create caramels, gummies, pralines and toffees. But it's the chocolate that keeps people coming back for more. The shop uses 100% cocoa and cocoa butter and no artificial preservatives. The chocolate comes in individual pieces, bark or pieces and white, dark or milk chocolate is available.

Viru Centre

Viru Valjak
Tallinn 10111, Estonia
372-610-1444
www.virukeskus.com

This 4-floor center is located downtown and offers something for any shopper's needs, from books to fashion outlets, to department stores. They also offer beauty items, gift stores, designer stores such as Calvin Klein, accessories, and children's toys.

They are open from 8 a.m. to 9 p.m. daily. Visit their web site for updated information on fashion and cultural events that they present on the premises, as well.

Town Hall Square

Raekojaplats 11
Tallinn 10111, Estonia
372-631-4860
www.kaeapteek.ee

There are many shops, cafes and market vendors in this area, which is part of Old Town. The shops offer antiques, souvenirs, handicrafts, wool, candy, bath items and dolls among many other specialties. But one of the highlights is the Town Hall Pharmacy which is the oldest in Tallinn. Even the Russian Tsar used to order items from the pharmacy, whose web site and phone number are listed above.

They carry many herbs and natural remedies as well as more traditional pharmacy items and are open from 10 a.m. to 6 p.m. Tuesday through Saturday. Ironically, this is also the first place where the candy delicacy of marzipan was made and even today they periodically hold marzipan-making classes and demonstrations.

TALLINN TRAVEL GUIDE

Printed in Great Britain
by Amazon.co.uk, Ltd.,
Marston Gate.